Moon Writing

Poems

Betti E. Kahn

Teaneck, New Jersey

MOON WRITING ©2022 Betti E. Kahn. All rights reserved. No part of this book may be used or reproduced in any manner whatsoever without written permission except in the case of brief quotations embodied in critical articles and reviews.

Published by Ben Yehuda Press
122 Ayers Court #1B
Teaneck, NJ 07666

http://www.BenYehudaPress.com

To subscribe to our monthly book club and support independent Jewish publishing, visit https://www.patreon.com/BenYehudaPress

Jewish Poetry Project #22   http://jpoetry.us

Ben Yehuda Press books may be purchased at a discount by synagogues, book clubs, and other institutions buying in bulk. For information, please email markets@BenYehudaPress.com

Cover illustration by Betti E. Kahn

ISBN13 978-1-953829-17-7

22 23 24 / 10 9 8 7 6 5 4 3 2 1   20221121

*I dedicate these poems to my country,
the United States of America,
where First Amendment rights are
essential parts of our constitution.*

*I dedicate these poems to the continuance of our
citizenry getting to know each other more and
more, so that we can honestly honor each other
in the exercise of those stated freedoms.*

Contents

WE ARRIVE WITH OUR KNAPSACKS FULL OF STORIES

We Arrive with Our Knapsacks Full of Stories	2
A Tale of Two	3
Inside View	4
The Anti-Dance of Lot's Wife	5
Momentous Miriam	6
Did Miriam Stutter Too?	7
Moses, Through the Cloud	8
Blood Line	9
The Binding	10
Imperfect Tools	12
Job's Tears	13
Biblical Tense Unknotted	14

ALMOST SPEECHLESS, SHE SAYS

Almost Speechless, She Says	16
No Fear, No Thing	17
Day's Lesson on The Beach	18
Another Way to Be Naked	19
Dayenu—Dream of More than Enough	20
Some of Us Need to Break our Necks	21

T-MAIL

Flower Shop Prayer	24
Alef Bet	25
Moon Writing	26
Learning Hebrew	27
Baruch, Blessed—Seven Ways to Pray	28
Blessed Is The Name	29
Torah Study, Trupping the Light Fantastic	30
Time	31
A Walk Home from The River	32
T-Mail	33

LEGACY

Lost and Found	36
My Dad's Death	37
On the Death of my Brother, Isadore Elfman, October 22, 2006	38
Sent From My Brother Joseph, Six Days Buried, He— Puzzler of Intricate Dreams	39
My Brother Abe—	40
My Brother Reuben, During His Final Illness—	41
Three Sisters	42

LATE SUMMER

Late Summer	44
Death—Closed and Open	45
How Dirty Is Death?	46
On Mourning—November, 2006	47
Death	48
Celebrants	49
Ritual	50
Dr. L. with Stethoscope and Pen	51
Everything	52

PEACE

Sunrise	56
When Finally I Saw I Had No Time	57
Into the Dance	58
A Few Unanswered Questions	59
She Was Grandmother, *Bubbi*	60

LIMEN SERIES

Decoding	62
Dream of The Chant, The Dance, Music of The Cloud	63
Knowing Our Dreams	64
The Compassionate Shorthand of Dreams	65
Not Dreaming	66
Eleven Days Before the New Moon	67
Vision	68
Moon, Seed, Sunflower	69
At Sleep Level	70
Uni-verse	71

Acknowledgements	72
About the Author	74

PART I

—

WE ARRIVE WITH OUR KNAPSACKS FULL OF STORIES

We Arrive with Our Knapsacks Full of Stories

   an infinite variety of plots, characters,
mid-points and endings. The trouble is we don't know,

at first, which character we are. Discovering that persona,
our play unfolds. Many Abels, Cains, Josephs—

we find ourselves Matriarchs, Patriarchs—all
impeccably flawed. Outrageous events occur.

The sea splits. Adam's rib gives birth to Eve.
Abraham ready to sacrifice his and Sarah's only son,

very late begotten. Blind men see enough
to bless the younger. Deceit prevails, kind of—each of us

simmering in our own stew. Whom shall we become?
How to reach home? The wise bywords: *Listen*   *Love*

Choose life!   Do good for all co-travelers
in each scene, seeing in them the strangers we were,

forgiving our proclivity to err—before the last curtain call.
We gratefully acknowledge, receive Audience.

*

K-nowledge
N-ot
A-lways
P-erceived, Practiced

S
A
C-red

K-nowledge
S-ings

Betti E. Kahn

A Tale of Two

Hard to believe   that story
that Eve would have locked herself
in such a cage   Sounds like storyteller's
spiel   So nonchalant the release

a dead giveaway   *Interesting* Father
to let go so easily   Sure   He   (this is
not a Mother's tale)   didn't know
how Eve got there   *Uh huh*   Next

He'll want to deliver this piece of land
a paradise   The upkeep is high
Always the work   the planning
not easy   But the gift of life always good

So she's out now   A little new at being
here   Free   and she knows it.

Inside View

Here she is—she feels spilled
from that ticklish place

into the arms of first dawn.
What is

that rosy glow? She can't help
but smile at the fanning upward

spread of (What's it called?) *light*.
That gold-red ball thrown into

her wide open line of sight
exudes a warmth. She feels it tingle

her skin, or is that Adam holding her
hand? She sees the rose and

etrog blossom from the kiss
of its rays. Snake and kitten loll and

play in the garden. Something called
a *day* goes by, travels with shine

until, like Sabbath candle spark and
echo, it whispers—*Rest*.

The Anti-Dance of Lot's Wife

"Love ya," Lot's
wife mutters. But she
must turn away, look
back.
                        Then her family
had a hold on her,
a neck-crackling, arm-twisting
grasp. All her intuition
clasped her heart—then
fled—for fear, for fear.
                        Missing them
in the backward view
her eyes cast a yearning
glance.
                        But the snapshot
shuttered lens, white-spotted
in an instant snow-flaked,
salt-caked all memory.
Till pillared into her next life
she could recall
days, moments with
her children.

They would ask
        Remember when…?
and she could not. Then knew
she had not been there,
                had not been most
of her life. She wondered, *What
had been her destination?* Seeing
the blurred yesterdays now.
Un-named, even by the Un-nameable,
it seemed— for years
she had known
        the taste of tears

Momentous Miriam

> *Then Miriam, the prophetess, Aaron's sister took a timbrel in her hand, and all the women went out, after her in dance with timbrels.*
>
> *Exodus 15:20-21*

To keep the marchers moving
the water dance that Miriam led
wove near enough surrounding wells
to keep all tongues from parching.

Parsing words of timbrel songs,
her syncopated rhythms—
just wild enough to spring
our hearts from place to place—

just calm enough to soothe
our quavering breath. No mischief,
but a mission of *merci*, her goal.
Thankful for every drop she knew

was promised. Thankful
that we had chosen, dared to trust
to leave our bondage.
                    Thankful, she danced.

Did Miriam Stutter Too?

We do not know, do not hear her voice
alongside her brother.

We do know they quarreled
at Meribah—and the waters healed.

Did she wear a veil too, as Moses
placed upon himself after he heard God?

Was silence her friend? Did it dance
out of her, unannounced

timbrel, pronouncing freedom with each step?

Moses, Through the Cloud

No, he said to God.
I am not worthy.
How can I be?
I cannot speak.

My voice is broken.
It is many parts of light.
My doubt, a prism
of scattered hue.

Vocal cords, holy sound flow
You have given me wavers.
They are desert dry.
Since I was a child, I fear

every word I utter
will come stumbling out of me—
that they will strike rocks
in sheer frustration.

Breathe, Breathe, Breathe
You say as I draw close to me
the air and mist
of Your Cloud.

Blood Line

Boils. Boiling blood
streams through veins.
Ubiquitous pain, as locusts
unrelenting, even the frogs taunt
hopping as we, fear-frozen cannot.

Bodies weary from
being flogged, burdened.
Bricks clog the lungs. Walls
of others' design—monuments
to what?

*

Then flowing robes, sandaled feet.
A holy cloud. Could it embrace
not just the brilliant leading heart,
but the halting tongue, the hesitant
step?

That first one into the crossing
tumultuous. Sounds of sea mammals
close by but we, led—miraculous—
separately tread on dry land.
Swift breath and sea roars, shouts.

*

Awed silence.
Old and young
woman and man, believer
and not, we move.   Our souls
transported by promise.
Manna and trials to come.

      Soon

the first-born's child
hears his father's chant.

The Binding

We were one, made of the same stuff. She bound me to her
with little stitches, showed me the even in-out motion around
the whole outline of the doll's dress turned inside out, made right
again when we finished, like that time I felt my body curve in
on me, spilling inside out, yearning toward a dark, starry sky.

> *And I lay on that altar for many years, shivered*
> *in the dry heat, deserted. She did what women did,*
> *had children, seven. The landscape barren after*
> *she died. She and I too young for that journey.*
>
> *Trust severed when she left, yet it seemed forever*
> *bound to that place where great powers were and*
> *still were not. Not the cloud draped for the multitude's*
> *view, but a void. No voice except a small lullaby*
> *I sang myself; "to pray" in Hebrew a reflexive verb.*

The doll's dress, my first and only doll, enlarged in my mind
through the years, became fit for her and she the Goddess
became the vision. Odd reversal, as Mother Sarah, pushed out
of the Bible picture, so my father unceremoniously, despite the gift
of life, *Chaim* his name, was pushed out of the door, daily life.

> *The cords on my wrists tightened at first by absence.*
> *Her mind bent on its own search. My stuttered faith pierced*
> *the air. For a long time I faulted her for bringing me to this place.*
>
> *And he, singer of joy and sorrow, silently left me alone.*
> *So I was here, listening to every wind's whisper. Hyper-aware*
> *of the night, moon-drift, morning dew, the viper, its sting.*

The stern voice of God telling parents to stronghold, strangle
the life from the child did not occur in the house of doll-making.
She felt that stricture later, outside her home. The other heart-
clutching was subtler, but there. The child, acting-parent, learned to
hold on too long to hope, to despair.

*The letting go, the sacrifice took time. In not-knowing—
how I came to know, even in dreams, heart messages sent by the wind.
Cloud pictures spelled her love for me. The strength of her sea and
stream-loving body remembered in ocean's embrace. A presence felt
but not seen, like the steadying absence of the moon. Shadow and sun
drops meld as The Great Voice enunciates: "Do not raise your hand.
Do not pass the child through fire."*

Imperfect Tools

Oddly comforting   Isaiah   perhaps mad

scorches me with anger.   Impatient

with my hypocrisy.   Yet bending to point

with sword turned into plough shares.

How to feed the many   hungry mouths?

Job's Tears

She wore Job's tears around her neck
nearly all her life. Job's relative,
she did not know how to reach
the filled gourd. The boils erupted
fatigue at the mocking stretched out
forever. Impatient questioner, she
dared to think there might be answers,
shibboleths written in the sky.

She tried deciphering the moon
sun and stars. And in
their multiplicity found one
thing sure—Given numbers, letters
words may change, evade our view;
yet all the while, to ask, divinely pure.

Biblical Tense Unknotted

There   Is

                No
ti   me.

Like

                the *present.*

Meaning

transcends
as hearts of

ONE   dreamed *Let us!*

                stunningly
placed.

                I accept

    this golden gift.

Part 2

—

ALMOST SPEECHLESS, SHE SAYS

Almost Speechless, She Says

> *Aish: Hebrew for fire,*
> *beginning with alef*
> *and a vowel.*

Alef—the sound
making no sound

    The beginning

        before the beginning

        The first of The Mystery's
        names starting with
        the almost sound
        she needs to say

Her eyes barely open
        almost fearless   almost sure

She gains impetus to move   like *alef* along with a vowel
        and the song she now hears

        ocean wave morphing into spirited salt spray
reaching the shore

While the strings so long not heard   their singing kept from her

        play music's fire   *aish*
        Its flame burns patiently
        does not harm

            The cello   almost her favorite
            lifelong   and then there's   drum
            that rhymes with heartbeat

                horn   that helps her
                today   breathe
                strength   into her lungs.

Betti E. Kahn

No Fear, No Thing

Dear God I don't even know how to spell   how to say your name   let alone
what it means   Is it *yud hay vov hay*   the unpronounceable?

Is it Lord   Lady   of river flow?   Is war   your imperfect
clutter of cruelty   or ours?   We partner   chaos or calm
Do I get the picture   stand tall   share breath   like hair-of-*god*-trees?

Flood of sounds   swooshed into black holes   Forget time
that mountainous climb   forward   back   all   at once
Force of   song   brainwaves   light   ocean purr and roar

If there were   only   story   sunrise-dance   no more than a chance
God knows   to try again   would it be enough   to quell our trembling?
Enough   to laugh-cry   see the sparkle on spider web   hear warbler trill?

**Tetragrammaton:* the Hebrew word for God consisting of the four letters *yud, hay, vov, hay,* transliterated consonantally usually as *YHVH,* now pronounced as *Adonoi* or *Elohim* in substitution for the original pronunciation forbidden since the 2nd or 3rd century BCE.

Day's Lesson on The Beach

We called to the sun.
It shone, electric

beaming through us,
glints from the ocean.

Know that dolphins
will come, swim by

while we watch. See
the kite-drawn skiers

skim surf. Strong
pelicans too, on the sand.

Some stand on one foot
as Rabbi Hillel, long ago

taught us, ancient wisdom
all we need to know.

Another Way to Be Naked

                                      Stripped of all labels—
my Jewish soul within

shorn of the thorned crown of Chosenness.
       (The way of new Commandments so hard,
       a loving Parent-God said *You are special.*
       The confidence to do and be—wishfully
       instilled.)

I am weary of feinting, dodging bullets
aimed by those with ill-perceiving eyes, half-closed,
crossed—evilly with a view toward my obliteration—
as if that done deed would cure their woes.

I am weary of the hair-cloth others wrap around me,
a coat of many colors, inside-out. Its threads of too rich,
too smart, too holier-than-thou, too noisy, too isolate
rub my skin raw.

       I can almost imagine the soft breeze caressing
my bare breast, spine, feet—as I'd walk a neutral path.
No name-calling
                            for I would have no name,
                            just   *The Name.*

*Ha Shem, The Name, another designation for God.

Dayenu—Dream of More than Enough

Every woman man child   each a poem   heard.
Laments lauds shouts   their daily dance   seeing
hearing.   Pride   greed's cloak   thrown off.

Silver platters of clean streams reflect blue   sky.
Air filled with particles of love   all the knitted-ness
desired. Oceans free of our debris   sing to me

healed   as we carry   into the world   all
tools given   received by us   I with my paint brush
and ladder   you   with your pail and tar.

**Dayenu,* Hebrew for *enough*. The name of a traditional Passover song signifying that if The Creator had "only" given us the great gifts of life, freedom etc. "that would have been "enough."

Some of Us Need to Break our Necks

> *Hebrew Midrash: An angel presses a finger*
> *over each newborn's lips (thus the indentation*
> *beneath our nose) to initially keep mysterious our*
> *life's purpose—only for each to rediscover.*

     to allow our souls more breath—
our realness to bless the world.

Some need to hold our necks straighter
supported by the healthy spine given us—

hold our heads high to feel the caress
of holy whisper or hearty shout,

whatever has been confessed to us
secretly by our Creator, impressed

beneath our very noses, as the midrash
tells. Seekers all— we need to smell death

to fully enjoy life's aromas.
Difficult if olfactory is dulled.

     So touching, seeing the rose
     hearing the silk of its opening

          tasting its hips in sacred tea
          is my loving task

               to compensate that sleepy sense.
               How fortunate to be stiff-necked

                    and humbled, lowly—
                    raised up

Part 3
—
T-MAIL

Flower Shop Prayer

Freesia, three for six dollars—
the South Street shop ad reads.

Rust, butterscotch, rose-peach,
their petals preach a silent *trope*,

the Hebrew rhythm and melody
pattern for scripture.

                        She hopes to
learn a portion, her portion of

Torah to recite as belated
bat mitzvah—plus—jubilee year!

She prays for the bloom's
                          eloquence.

Alef Bet

                I inscribe those letters

inside veins   nerves and arteries   desert rhythms
blooming   oases found

First the spoken word   the jaw   good ole reliable
temporal mandibular joint   unlocks

More slowly   the soul   like praying mantis
accustomed to feeding on-the-face-of-things

Fear of *Not-Enough*   that tough sly bird reappears
Gently   feather by feather   I will soothe him

move my hands in flow signs   sing
as first the braying parrot   with fiery wings

                then soul and I take sacred flight.

Moon Writing

                Circle of celestial ink   milk white   silk light
its wane and waxing   jibe with ocean flow and ebb

to cause the slightest hair to blow   in wind or wave
Whether this hair   caressed by lover or mother

singled out of a plate of food   picked up with distaste
discarded   the cook blamed silently or outright   when

it was that sky coin's doing   plain and simple   She sings
her silent song   I listen   listen   Surely *the moon woke me*

shone in at this full time   its light on my eyes   and on
the three-&-a-half by three-&-a-half foot canvas   of three

figures above the bed   where it (Yes, the moon)
writes Hebrew letters   superimposes them on the nudes

I painted there a long time ago

                               It writes the silent *alef*
the one you need before you can say anything   *yud* the tenth

bringing change   *hei*   the baring present moment   *vov*
the connector   and prints late at night for me   while I learn

this age-old tongue   a map of the DNA of the world
                    and my part in breathing it out   and in.

Betti E. Kahn

Learning Hebrew

My brain feels like half a commercial
can of alphabet noodle soup, without
benefit of clear, fresh water yet added
to it. The *alef bet*, Hebrew, a compressed
language. That's it.
                                           Not enough space
for noodling around. The three-lettered
root concise, clear, precisely what it
says. Each vowel —exact in its changing
location. We are promised signs.
Then Poof!
see them disappear before our very
eyes. *Ee. Ah.* Endings singular, plural—to say
nothing of masculine, feminine, position.
Verbs, nouns, adjectives, prepositions making
me (is that *us?*) feel un-conjugated.

I hear my rabbi's voice. Hear her chant the
trupp, to teach each symbol's sound, name.
Dargah, zarkah-- more terms to learn beside
the *alef bet* stir me to study day & night.
Engage the right & what is left of me. Make me

                                    feel this wholly.

Baruch, **Blessed—Seven Ways to Pray**

Baruch from the Hebrew root
bend the knee   so   to   for and   from you
do I
         plow the field   partnering

dance my limbs here there
bent on love and mystery   straight
from the core

            faint fall prostrate with grief
            over war's continuous knell   then rise
            march in protest   words of heaven   hell

recall within my bones baby's crawl
precursor to the walk   How learning spurs
the pace   now slow   now quickened grace

            entranced   climb hill and mountain
            in soft air   look up
            in awe of time's humbling canopy

Blessed
bend the knee.

Betti E. Kahn

Blessed Is *The Name*

                                                        Seeing the invisible
Power   like and unlike opossum   mountain peak   x-ray   DNA
we connect   begin to recognize each other   each self

between us   know a little about each other   enough to question
ask a favor   argue with   test   and especially   to praise.

By the time we laud we are in awe   hold a loosely woven basket
of fear   kissing the mysterious   as if it had appeared one autumn day
in yellow rain slicker red rubber boots   to walk with us in wet woods.

We want to face it   declare our love full of grace-light.   The prize
so sweetly shared   even when we fall   tripping over our flaws.

Torah Study, *Trupping* the Light Fantastic

Dance—the letters
to their own
hand-swaying tune.

To know these
steps, words a
lifetimes' pursuit.

Late-comer to this
world of truth.
Blazing light—

before me. My feet
grounded in sound
sense rhythms of

these gem-cut words.
May I rise
with their holy flow.

Time

    holy
            word.

Quick-spoken or slow.

Delicate bridge I must
attend to every step. And when I do
I fly. Pass by peripheral sights.

Feel the pomegranate seed or bitters
in every tread. Not dread but feat of faith
required. Once mired in last year's tunneled
view.
      This second
          time
                attuned.

A Walk Home from The River

Waterfall trills its tune
To cold-splashed river.
Two *chaverim* and I swing hands
Held high along the hum of road.

We chant *Shema* to sky—
Full throats and hearts
In three-part round,
V'ahavta along the way.

Sing—green leaves, each one
Repeated letter of the *alef bet*—
Small bird I cannot see,
Only hear your song.

*chaverim: friends
*Shema: the watchword of the Jewish faith: Hear, Oh Israel. The Eternal is our God, The Eternal One alone!
**V'Ahavta*: And you shall love The One, your God
*alef bet: alphabet

T-Mail

Torah says—
Sing me.
Make meaning clear.

Here
      O, Israel
      Am I.

Part 4
—
LEGACY

Lost and Found

The sound of a solitary goose woke me
this Sunday morning,
        a plea, repeated bleating.

Out the apartment window on the large lawn.
a wandering, slight goose
        twists her head left right left right.

Again, and again her frightened cry
reminds me of my early days, when eight
        a motherless child, I feel like

I want to gently hold her, enfold her
until her mother returns.
        I keep looking for the parent until,

not the sole lonely sound, but there she is
I see her large, flapping wings.
        The adult appears
                        hovering above
                          April air

My Dad's Death

        happened when the second lightning bolt struck

eight years after my mom had passed on.

Another quivering mind-limit, crisscrossed.

Confused custom showed me I had been right / wrong:

Jews generally show only a closed coffin.

Somehow my father's was open.

The shock of seeing my father "funeral parlor dead" remained

with me forever. The mask which I faced as I looked

into the open coffin only reinforced my wishes. "He hasn't died.

He hasn't died. He hasn't died."

On the Death of my Brother, Isadore Elfman, October 22, 2006

    Death's eye peers

    erases *is, will be*

    echoes in reverse the contraction of birth

    divides the Red Sea of life from itself.

Breakwaters
spill stuttered clouds
speaking certainty

though we wish
not to hear
the wordless tango

not to see
the persistent partner
and feel the lead grasp

that dislocates
breath
and speech, close embrace.

    True, your name, Yitzchak, means laughter. Did that
    help traverse the hell of illness, hear the beat of earth's
    thud on the coffin, journeyman's jive and Haydn,

    you'd have chosen, accompaniment for the trek?
    The fall from limbo, gravest peace, but lilting. Your will
    to write; your eyes, youthful pitching arm shine.

    Heart-rain making mud so we may feel
    soul's touch before it dries
    and wind lifts it from sight.

Betti E. Kahn

**Sent From My Brother Joseph, Six Days Buried, He—
Puzzler of Intricate Dreams**

I walked across his body, he, a teenager,
young adult. He offered to bridge a high
and low terrain. He knew I was shy
of falling from the balcony. His friend,
a lawyer-poet-artist who let me view
his work, said good-bye, joking, hinting

for me to leave.

My daughter, who chatted wisely and happily
about the day, was with me. Usually afraid
of heights, she showed no fear. Instead,
she pointed, offered me cues: *Step here,*

or here.

Outside the elegant apartment, the land-
scape, classic—with a clean, shiny glow.
I stepped across the offered body-bridge,
descended onto a pink, stucco patio-
courtyard. Shaded by day by gingko and
lantern-lit by night. A sailboat waited for me
on the turquoise sea, just outside the

latched gate.

My Brother Abe—

                                                kind   fun   bright—
served in World War II in Italy   told me later
of his regimen   climbing the Alps   on horseback

carrying rifles   all of which he'd never done before
Brothers Iz and Joe also served   but in Japan and France
I don't know the details   only that Abe suffered most

what came to be known as PTSD   He received some
treatment   was able to continue his government job
had a girlfriend   They never married   He lived alone

stayed in touch with family   Suddenly we got this call
Abe whom I loved   always will   died of a heart attack
during the night   He was 54 years young.

My Brother Reuben, During His Final Illness—

his brain, cluttered.
Memories nowhere, everywhere—disjointed.
To friends, "Where have we met? Can't place you."

His smile, sunbeams on the murky lake, tries to locate
chameleon-like faces, names to their secure habitats.

Later, in the hospital room, he asks a half-question,
jokingly of his son who fetched him a hard candy
to soothe his dry throat. "Okay, so it's recess now"?

*

Trying to reminisce I ask "Ruby, do you remember
being a boy scout? He smiled, quickly asked, "Where?"

I related being four and, with my dad, proudly
seeing my thirteen-year-old brother march near
City Hall in the Thanksgiving Day Parade.

My hero, Ruby, who, when a kid offered to take my place
to go to a foster home, Mom too ill to take care of all of us.

At college, both parents gone by then,
he rescued me with emergency funds. Later
I'd go to him for thoughts on all life's quandaries.

*

His smile flashes into the beige-colored hospital room,
as Mozart, his favorite, soothes, provides music's lattice.

A mute TV ripples gentle land and seascapes.
His geography—wife, daughter, granddaughter. A family
bridge. He calls their names, mistakes their voices with the nurses'.

Next day brings bodily improvement. Now, rehab, walks
in the hall, physical therapy part of his daily map.

More smiles. Lucid or confused—
Ruby's never fading country of the heart.

Three Sisters

                We were
yawed by tides   unaware
Tides strong as family ties
hidden as love   unending

      Caring   three sisters.

PART 5
—
LATE SUMMER

Late Summer

The jelly fish   and its late summer sting
I try to avoid   tells me with its tangled
tentacles   we're not meant to penetrate
all transparencies   can not always see

when death's innards reveal themselves
dare to dance before my view
Nothing to do but swim   swim and play
Taste the salt wish

Haven't the waves always veered me from
a piercing?   If the slant among the seaweed
strikes my dreams

if I do not know   believe   that I am quick
then cursed   self-cursed   not only stung
but swallowed   by worse.

Death—Closed and Open

The shutting away from

                one whose face

I can't forget   your eyes

      tried   so hard and did succeed

where others   would have failed

peace   of angels you deserve

now open   hope for you

        show clear   the way the heart must.

How Dirty Is Death?

Blood spilling out of orifice   Is there gumminess
to it   or is that so   only if we are alive and maybe
we cut ourselves   not off for good   or forever
Rather   the sticky nicks   and paper cuts
that fortune   or our inner organs   stumbling
send us   Mending   built right in.

Are some deaths more unclean   messier than
the natural variety   Mangled limbs from stupidly
large SUV's   The giant lugs oblivious to the havoc
they cause   The bitter fruits   seed spilled
for needs   for gain   No clear-cut way out.

On Mourning—November, 2006

The poet: "I carried the dead
on my back for many years."

How long?
How long must I aid the gravediggers?

The clarinet wedding music starts
me tapping my feet in spite
of the black mourning ribbon I wear.

They play a scissors-dance, a *sher*—cutting
what—a Jewish jazzed-up version of marriage,

or end game memories of white pine boxes
carrying too many loved ones into the earth—
sacred, but no more foot-tapping there.

I tell my Abandonment—childhood hauntings—
"Get off my back—you dead man.
Heave your hairy chest away from mine."

Catgut violin song clambers into the torn
worn case given me by a favorite teacher.
"Play by ear. The music will read itself."
I listen. I clear my throat.

Can I stand on one foot like the angels?

That's all they have—don't need
two. Wings are what they wear.

Wings help carry the dead, lift them.
Their wings free, flutter.

I need not do the job alone.

Death

          that gray bitch
haunts me
tore mother father each
sister brother from earshot.

Family before them
gored, dumped
into pits somewhere
in Lithuania?

I want to swat that hound
clear the road of it
know nearly useless
tears.

Celebrants

Father's waltz   Mother's two-step

sister's shimmy and brother's swing

Death's shadow   always ready

to cut in.

Ritual

So many voids
the world full of them.
Unknown relatives

in mass graves.
Or did they survive?
Still lost to family here.

Their bones in the vast
ritual of music un-played,
like violin bow taut.

All our unstrung lives
saved by utterance.

Dr. L. with Stethoscope and Pen

He stands
or sits at white metal desk listening, takes notes

queries, offers clue of what to do
to remedy this, that. Routine exam complete,

My quandary speaks itself:
Dr. L., How do you separate

yourself from

death? His dark, Indian eyes
fully focus on me.

My words jump out: Four illnesses,
three terminal

have clawed life
these past two weeks.

Dr. L. replies, Learning to turn that doorknob shut
takes doing. Still his hand

touches his heart to say It's not easy.
So time, I ask, will teach that lesson?

I leave, shielded by a practice
glass bubble -

Everything

1.
One day   the cat

sat on a chair

got up

walked under the table

sat near me & YELLED a meow louder than multi-cell-phone signals.

I knew he wasn't hungry. He lapped milk

so coolly.   He knew there'd always be enough.

That night   I could not hear his purr in

or outside.   No scratching like the all-powerful

slurping tea   at their parties   though Charlsie could

pose like them.   In a blink

he leaped from table top   to sofa arm   to hassock.   Crouched

flew again from oak floor to every height.

2.
Night prances held not a sip of fear.   His leap-dance

transparent. I caught sight of his antics once when I couldn't sleep.

Other times when I wrote   deadlines   lifelines?

he'd walk across computer keyboard   want petting.   If only

Betti E. Kahn

I'd been on financial websites   he'd have hedged me a fortune.

My own Single Payer Plan   he'd climb   curl and purr   on my lap

if I had a tummy ache   or on my leg   if a cramp.   His pureness knew

when love was right   (pearl or cur)   stretching across laps.

3.
He'd watched the house being built

treasured wood and careful fire   aware of every scent in every corner.

He went outside   but stayed close by, licking his paws

beneath the weeping cherry tree   at home with himself.

Travel(to the vet) Charlsie'd veto by his long strong un-shy YELL.   This the same

woman who clued me in he wasn't a *he*. This feline given to me

by a friend who'd named it Charles (I added *ie*.)   My last cat in pre-school days

i never checked it out. Tabbies are usually female   so Charlsie   post exam and tests

Voila!   Charlsina.

4.
She used a special door from the kitchen to the basement

the wood cut at floor level   rounded-arch-shaped.   This

the well-known tabby-route to her litter box.

My grandson's allergies the reason I had to find a new home for Charlsina.

Moon Writing

(She who took to the tango   almost *danced!*)   I found a gentle doctor.

It was love at first sight between them.   Charlsina and I

said our farewell.

5.
One day when

it's time for Charlsina to meet death   I imagine

her confidently walking through that archway   walking   dancing?

a line

whatever
the length or breadth of it may be.

PART 6
—
PEACE

Sunrise

The last true lover,
life (or that other)
whispers:

Embrace
July sunrise
for soon winter comes.

Tend the showy rose,
gray-green lamb's ear.
Hear curled petals open.

In mid-August,
when salt ocean currents
shift, swim strong.

Love
to walk in autumn winds,
feel their questions wail.

Wait for the reply.

When Finally I Saw I Had No Time

                         to write about death
but for sure   time for death   it occurred to me it would
happy   *happen*   clearly I saw   in a way
wildly unknown to me

                      I could learn tears
learn the taste of bitter herbs and sweet   the honey mix
of husband   kids   Senses lit   be with family and friends
know they'd know how much I'd miss them

                  write with all the heart left to me
for good!   only hope to un-smack death's lips   lift my
lid one last leap into Rothko   tango   hugs   kiss
this world   work to keep alive   its high wire balancing act.

Into the Dance

                                                            close-embraced,
the silk cape of tango flings itself about us.

Quince, its taste foreign to me, but of the rose family,
sings into my nostrils, takes me to a ridge of acacia trees

where the leaves and small yellow buds blend rhythms and rivers.
Ochos, side step pivots, ankles hugging snugly

sketch infinity, lace a map, yet untraveled.
Ocean tides and stars clear, restore us to joined islands of each other.

Today's dance, promise of bell chime hems and sewn pomegranates
ushers in the Sabbath Bride. Sweet red wine, wheat alchemized

to bread set on a pure white cloth. Candle glow treats us to
second sight as souls rise—a night of grace under lapis sky.

A Few Unanswered Questions

Finger tip touch
across war-stressed
lines of intelligence.
When will you arrive—
by ship or plane?

Who or what is hidden
in the rubble of lives?
Felled buildings,
telephone wires,
tangled knots each day.

How is the victory
of a vanquished heart
acknowledged? Who is
captive? Who is free?
Where—

parietal lobe, pulse, flesh,
home—does peace reside?

She Was Grandmother, *Bubbi*

    the first time she heard
the piercing rhythm of the *shofar*— from her own lips.
Not an intake of breath, but a wonderful

exhale, baby-learning-language (a raspberry) release;
the aperture, not surrounding her lips. Mouth,
plainly focused on the small open space of ram's horn.

A meeting of holy air, relaxed into the abundant
curve, that spirals outward again
to change silence to sound.

        Tekia, - - - *Truah*-------
        The blasts broken up, divided.
        Their meaning, ancient code.

We're born in light. We grow up. We die. Do we become
all our mothers, fathers, brothers, sisters—all angels
now? *Tekia Gedola*——We go out grandly.

The middle breaths—the ra-ta-ta-ta of our days,
its desire, gain, loss, hate, love—open, close.
When night comes, we let go, grow into this life, the next.

The song within us—all the breath we need—and more.

*The *shofar*, a ram's horn, is blown to welcome in the Jewish New Year.

Part 7

—

LIMEN SERIES

Decoding

1.
A beautiful canvas, as if with beveled edges
dropping off to somewhere.

Separate letters of the Hebrew alphabet, *fay, shin, pay*
sounds, hard to distinguish as endings,

high frequency, as our hearing fades.
They fall, float—our lives, each with its own message.

2.
Radiant mountain ridge, a chance at silence,
horses faithfully stepping past rocks.

Whatever came before this, erased in time.
The gentle rain and soft gray sky bless the day.

The last phase of the journey seeks and finds bright
sky-band. We cannot see its end, but the arc is clear.

Dream of The Chant, The Dance, Music of The Cloud

                              A man with a cello
walks down the deserted street.
Four steps behind, a woman,
with an ancient tambourine.

They arrive together at the green square,
       candles lighting their curved path
              dotted with urns of hibiscus.

Beneath a catalpa tree
they play music—tango, birdsong, &
blue jazz wail—while she chants & dances.

Listeners gather.
       Some—redheaded Jews
             wander in.

Others with straight black hair,
almond eyes. Still others
blond, eyes sky-blue.

They join in the dance as music floats above them.
       Dancers & musicians, enjoy each
             droplet of their perspiration, each breath.

A juggler appears from among them.
She teaches a new feat—to toss
the notes in the air, see their colors flaunt

themselves from every angle, retreat & re-appear.
       These folks do not compete
             for sound waves of strings & drum-like beat;

                                  do not fight
for strains that repeat & repeat.

Knowing Our Dreams

                    The bridge from sleep to waking.
In my backpack, a crinkled dream or two.

They are sprinkled cat food in my brain
food for the furry creature, tiptoeing there.

Was it a song I knew in childhood? Heaven sent
singing of Father, my son, or grandchild?

Travel to Umbria, four summers ago to meet poet-
friends, pen words seeped through thick stone

monastery walls, roosters crowing us into the day.
And last night, coming home from dance

as I crossed a wooden bridge, my thoughts,
from thin air drew up the name *Tabachnik.*

Foot and mind weary, I ask, Why that name?
No one I know. I muse, *Bach*, in German, brook.

Maybe, a capricious tune,
Ta means over? I smile.

I'm a cross-over-the-bridge-nik. Arriving home
in bed, I read briefly, before shutting my eyes.

The name *Tabachnik* appears in the first chapter.
Dream or awake—or is it all the same—

how much do we know, not know?
How much are we willing to ask, and asking,

                        what will be revealed?

Betti E. Kahn

The Compassionate Shorthand of Dreams

Color dream-shots slam, snap, brand themselves
onto my daily path—visual shout.

Searing meaning
melts boundary.

I am chair, river, stair & tree,
man, woman, child—elephant, snake
& doe. I speak every tongue—
I am family, friend, foe,

head-dressed devil & halo-ed saint.
I am future, past & now—
cat's healing purr
& dog of the heart.

I am—jealousy & love. All of the above
enfolded—Bound to those imprints.

I find delicious you & me—
(bulbs blink on, off)

letters say themselves
non-junk, all the atoms, molecules.

& junk*—lines of meaning meet along DNA
super clean highways, wooded byways.

---

* The once –thought "junk DNA" today is called noncoding DNA—Label for portions of a genome sequence.

Not Dreaming

Dark lashes weave and blend

Eye lids open   close

viewing and viewed   The source

of these orbs   mysterious

Wide   dazed

they simply appear   My closed lids

surprised   tired

automatic projection screen.

What do they mean   lenses

cleansed by oceans

Are they the brown, hazel and blue

of family, now gone to their rest

Or the green of survivors-and-not

teary   cataract-veiled

having seen violence of

the world

Eleven Days Before the New Moon

Swallowing the world
spitting it out whole.

Smelling the light
not knowing it. Then

dance steps rinse onto
old washboard's ripple.

In her sleep
the sweet cat croons.

Vision

An eye—
opens its rose petal lashes,

peers with knowing,
blinks, re-enters its cave

A gift, seeking synapses—
pomegranate-shaped

seeded in loam that gives
and receives naked mystery.

And like the moon in its phases,
its temporary veil winks

bloom, constant
reappearance. Soft earth

gives birth to second sight.

Moon, Seed, Sunflower

Night eyes and dream

many-colored

coat to wear   all day.

At Sleep Level

                        the way
the body can't do without the coast
into dreams   at the level place
wave meets shore   embraces
batters it   sand too
requires ocean.

                      On deserted isle
no footprints
zero creatures   trod its shifts
there   loudly do land
and sea   call to each other.

                          Wave upon
dream foam   floating
inside images   eyes   letters
Hebrew and English alphabet
mountains   flora   fauna

                      Array of DNA
puzzling forms   odd   juxtaposed   all
singing in hieroglyphics   sea chant
till meaning appears   with dawn.

                    Then full and whisper
surf song
caresses dreamer   homeland.

Uni-verse

The Jews joke:
"Life is no more than a dream
but don't wake me up."
And dream means
"thing equals word."
So dream
and world are text.
And words are holy.
No joke.

The scientist said
"Our DNA components
are like letters each
making unique words"—
Ourselves
sacred sounds
some waiting to be spoken.

So scientist, Jews, world
all One—that wrote
and writes and will write.
And mind, itself
a scripture,
ciphering—
deciphers.

Acknowledgements

I'd like to thank the editors of the following journals, where some of these poems first appeared: Ritual: *Poetry Super Highway*, Holocaust Remembrance Day Poem; When I Finally Saw I Had No Time: *Poetry Ink, 20th Anniversary Anthology*; Eleven Days Before the New Moon: *Schuylkill Valley Journal*; A Few Unanswered Questions: *Schuylkill Valley Journal*; Into the Dance: *Concordance*; She Was Grandmother, Bubbi: *Bridges, Jewish Feminist Journal*.

*

I'd like to thank a few wonderful people: Vivian Schirn, Rabbi Emeritus of Or Hadash, a Reconstructionist Congregation, 1983- 2001, and Joshua Waxman, rabbi of Or Hadash, 2003-2019—both of whom helped me with various poems in this collection.

Rabbi Vivian, as founding rabbi, had the responsibility of starting the congregation's existence, which she did with grace and love. She presided over my adult bat mitzvah (with 2 others from my class)— the last one she did before she retired—and performed our marriage ceremony, that of William Conrad and I, in 2012.

Rabbi Josh has, graciously and with deep insight, helped me sort through some puzzling life issues, has always been there when we've needed him, as well as led us, as a congregation, to various activist routes. He will be sorely missed by us, all at Or Hadash.

The marvelous traditions of holy intention, good will and the building of a community based on faith and love continue to thrive under the leadership of our current rabbi, with us since August 2019: Alanna Sklover. Or Hadash has been blessed by such good people.

*

I am grateful to the 34th Street Poet Collective, a group I've been meeting with since 1992, for their help with some of these poems.

I want to recognize, with much thanks, the always- there poet, teacher, friend— Leonard Gontarek, who has kindly aided me in editing some of these poems.

To Minter Krotzer and Hal Sirowitz, many thanks for their guidance in editing, help with poems, and the writing and publishing experience in general.

I am grateful for the good-humored patience and kind support that my late beloved husband William Conrad always provided. He passed away during the summer of 2021. He is sorely missed.

I want to thank my family of origin for being the wonderful people they all were. They, though differently oriented toward their Judaism, helped me find my own path, learn to deal with life and death, and find my own dreams. Finally, I feel huge thanks to both my sisters, Rose and Edith, each long gone, who helped raise me, when a child, during my mother's illness, and at Father's death. The cover I painted shows all the family women.

About the Author

Bettie. E. Kahn, a Pushcart Prize Nominee, is a recipient of both the Pennsylvania Council of the Arts and CBE grant, (the latter, Pew Trust Funded) among other awards. Her poems have appeared in *Harrisburg Review*, *Philadelphia Poets*, *Bridges: A Jewish Feminist Journal*, *Philadelphia Stories*, *Mad Poets Review*, *Schuylkill Valley Journal*, and *Tupelo Press Online Poetry Project* and many other journals.

A retired speech therapist, she lived in Wynnewood, Pennsylvania and taught poetry to intergenerational, interfaith and women's groups. She is an original member of the 34th Street Collective, and still very much enjoys this wonderful group of poets. She has authored three chapbooks: *Spring Apples Silver Birch* (Greenleaf Press), *Landscapes of Light* (Poets Wear Prada Press), and *Night Spark: The Zoe Poems* (Finishing Line Press).

She is also a retired Philadelphia public school teacher, and she has lived most of her life in various communities of Pennsylvania. In March 2022 she moved to Audubon, New Jersey, where she is now enjoying family and friends and acclimating herself to a rather busy environment. She hopes to publish more of her written work and with patience and "due diligence," she will enjoy accomplishing those goals.

The Jewish Poetry Project

Ben Yehuda Press

From the Coffee House of Jewish Dreamers: Poems of Wonder and Wandering and the Weekly Torah Portion by Isidore Century

"Isidore Century is a wonderful poet. His poems are funny, deeply observed, without pretension." – *The Jewish Week*

The House at the Center of the World: Poetic Midrash on Sacred Space by Abe Mezrich

"Direct and accessible, Mezrich's midrashic poems often tease profound meaning out of his chosen Torah texts. These poems remind us that our Creator is forgiving, that the spiritual and physical can inform one another, and that the supernatural can be carried into the everyday."
—Yehoshua November, author of *God's Optimism*

we who desire: Poems and Torah riffs by Sue Swartz

"Sue Swartz does magnificent acrobatics with the Torah. She takes the English that's become staid and boring, and adds something that's new and strange and exciting. These are poems that leave a taste in your mouth, and you walk away from them thinking, what did I just read? Oh, yeah. It's the Bible."
—Matthue Roth, author, *Yom Kippur A Go-Go*

Open My Lips: Prayers and Poems by Rachel Barenblat

"Barenblat's God is a personal God—one who lets her cry on His shoulder, and who rocks her like a colicky baby. These poems bridge the gap between the ineffable and the human. This collection will bring comfort to those with a religion of their own, as well as those seeking a relationship with some kind of higher power."
—Satya Robyn, author, *The Most Beautiful Thing*

Words for Blessing the World: Poems in Hebrew and English by Herbert J. Levine

"These writings express a profoundly earth-based theology in a language that is clear and comprehensible. These are works to study and learn from."
—Rodger Kamenetz, author, *The Jew in the Lotus*

Shiva Moon: Poems by Maxine Silverman

"The poems, deeply felt, are spare, spoken in a quiet but compelling voice, as if we were listening in to her inner life. This book is a precious record of the transformation saying Kaddish can bring. It deserves to be read. These are works to study and learn from."
—Howard Schwartz, author, *The Library of Dreams*

is: heretical Jewish blessings and poems by Yaakov Moshe (Jay Michaelson)

"Finally, Torah that speaks to and through the lives we are actually living: expanding the tent of holiness to embrace what has been cast out, elevating what has been kept down, advancing what has been held back, reveling in questions, revealing contradictions."
—Eden Pearlstein, aka eprhyme

Texts to the Holy: Poems
by Rachel Barenblat

"These poems are remarkable, radiating a love of God that is full bodied, innocent, raw, pulsating, hot, drunk. I can hardly fathom their faith but am grateful for the vistas they open. I will sit with them, and invite you to do the same."
—Merle Feld, author of A Spiritual Life.

The Sabbath Bee: Love Songs to Shabbat
by Wilhelmina Gottschalk

"Torah, say our sages, has seventy faces. As these prose poems reveal, so too does Shabbat. Here we meet Shabbat as familiar housemate, as the child whose presence transforms a family, as a spreading tree, as an annoying friend who insists on being celebrated, as a woman, as a man, as a bee, as the ocean."
—Rachel Barenblat, author, *The Velveteen Rabbi's Haggadah*

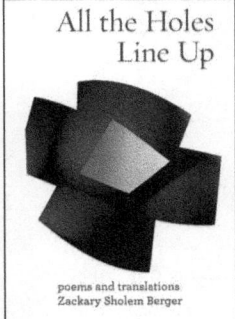

All the Holes Line Up: Poems and Translations
by Zackary Sholem Berger

"Spare and precise, Berger's poems gaze unflinchingly at—but also celebrate—human imperfection in its many forms. And what a delight that Berger also includes in this collection a handful of his resonant translations of some of the great Yiddish poets." —Yehoshua November, author of *God's Optimism* and *Two World Exist*

How to Bless the New Moon: The Priestess Paths Cycle and Other Poems for Queens
by Rachel Kann

"To read Rachel Kann's poems is to be confronted with the possibility that you, too, are prophet and beloved, touched by forces far beyond your mundane knowing. So, dear reader, enter into the 'perfumed forcefield' of these words—they are healing and transformative."
—Rabbi Jill Hammer, co-author of *The Hebrew Priestess*

Into My Garden: Prayers
by David Caplan

"The beauty of Caplan's book is that it is not polemical. It does not set out to win an argument or ask you whether you've put your tefillin on today. These gentle poems invite the reader into one person's profound, ambiguous religious experience."
—*The Jewish Review of Books*

Between the Mountain and the Land is the Lesson: Poetic Midrash on Sacred Community by Abe Mezrich

"Abe Mezrich cuts straight back to the roots of the Midrashic tradition, sermonizing as a poet, rather than ideologue. Best of all, Abe knows how to ask questions and avoid the obvious answers."
—Jake Marmer, author, *Jazz Talmud*

NOKADDISH: Poems in the Void
by Hanoch Guy Kaner

"A subversive, midrashic play with meanings—specifically Jewish meanings, and then the reversal and negation of these meanings."
—Robert G. Margolis

An Added Soul: Poems for a New Old Religion
by Herbert Levine

"These poems are remarkable, radiating a love of God that is full bodied, innocent, raw, pulsating, hot, drunk. I can hardly fathom their faith but am grateful for the vistas they open. I will sit with them, and invite you to do the same."
—Merle Feld, author of *A Spiritual Life*.

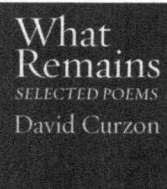
What Remains
by David Curzon

"Aphoristic, ekphrastic, and precise revelations animate What Remains. In his stunning rewriting of Psalm 1 and other biblical passages, Curzon shows himself to be a fabricator, a collector, and an heir to the literature, arts, and wisdom traditions of the planet."
—Alicia Ostriker, author of *The Volcano and After*

The Shortest Skirt in Shul
by Sass Oron

"These poems exuberantly explore gender, Torah, the masks we wear, and the way our bodies (and the ways we wear them) at once threaten stable narratives, and offer the kind of liberation that saves our lives."
—Alicia Jo Rabins, author of *Divinity School*, composer of *Girls In Trouble*

Walking Triptychs
by Ilya Gutner

These are poems from when I walked about Shanghai and thought about the meaning of the Holocaust.

Book of Failed Salvation
by Julia Knobloch

"These beautiful poems express a tender longing for spiritual, physical, and emotional connection. They detail a life in movement—across distances, faith, love, and doubt."
—David Caplan, author, *Into My Garden*

Daily Blessings: Poems on Tractate Berakhot
by Hillel Broder

"Hillel Broder does not just write poetry about the Talmud; he also draws out the Talmud's poetry, finding lyricism amidst legality and re-setting the Talmud's rich images like precious gems in end-stopped lines of verse."
—Ilana Kurshan, author of *If All the Seas Were Ink*

The Red Door: A dark fairy tale told in poems
by Shawn Harris

"THE RED DOOR, like its poet author Shawn C. Harris, transcends genres and identities. It is an exploration in crossing worlds. It brings together poetry and story telling, imagery and life events, spirit and body, the real and the fantastic, Jewish past and Jewish present, to spin one tale." —Einat Wilf, author, *The War of Return*

The Missing Jew: Poems 1976-2022
by Rodger Kamenetz

"How does Rodger Kamenetz manage to have so singular a voice and at the same time precisely encapsulate the world view of an entire generation (also mine) of text-hungry American Jews born in the middle of the twentieth century?"
—Jacqueline Osherow, author, *Ultimatum from Paradise* and *My Lookalike at the Krishna Temple: Poems*

The Matter of Families
by Robert Deluty

"Robert Deluty's career-spanning collection of New and Selected poems captures the essence of his work: the power of love, joy, and connection, all tied together with the poet's glorious sense of humor. This book is Deluty's masterpiece."
—Richard M. Berlin, M.D., author of *Freud on My Couch*

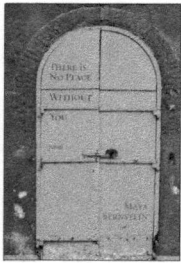

There Is No Place Without You
by Maya Bernstein

"Bernstein's poems brim with energy and sound, moving the reader around a world mapped by motherhood, contemplation, religion, and the effects of illness on the body and spirit. Her language is lyrical, delicate, and poised; her lens is lucid and original."
—Anthony Anaxagorou, author of *After the Formalities*

Torah Limericks
by Rhonda Rosenheck

"Rhonda Rosenheck knows the Hebrew Bible, and she knows that it can stand up to the sometimes silly, sometimes snarky, but always insightful scholarship packed into each one of these interpretive jewels."
—Rabbi Hillel Norry

Words for a Dazzling Firmament
by Abe Mezrich

"Mezrich is a cultivated craftsman: interpretively astute, sonically deliberate, and spiritually cunning."

—Zohar Atkins, author of *Nineveh*

www.ingramcontent.com/pod-product-compliance
Lightning Source LLC
LaVergne TN
LVHW041344080426
835512LV00006B/604